A POCKET GUIDE TO

SENSATIONAL
sex

A POCKET GUIDE TO

SENSATIONAL
sex

CARROLL & GRAF PUBLISHERS INC, NEW YORK

Published in 1997 by
Carroll & Graf Publishers, Inc.
260 Fifth Avenue
New York, NY 10001

Produced by Marshall Cavendish Books, London

ISBN 0 7867 0411 X

Library of Congress Cataloging-in-Publication Data is available

Printed and bound in Italy

CONTENTS

Condom Know-how

Gently unroll the condom one turn, with the roll on the outside, using hands that aren't moist from vaginal or penile juices. Squeeze the air from the empty tip (about ⅔ inch) and unroll, with your hand or your mouth, down your lover's erect penis. Choose the latex type, lubricated with the spermicide nonoxynol-9, rather than "natural" skin condoms, because the latter can let microscopic viruses pass through the rubber. Novelty condoms may be fun, but they're not reliable contraception.

Dispose of the condom, while your partner is still erect, in an ashtray or wastepaper basket placed by the bed beforehand. Do not dispose of the condom down the toilet, they can cause blockages.

Chapter One

The best sex is always founded on good communication between lovers. Set the scene for intimacy, and you are sure to increase your sexual pleasure.

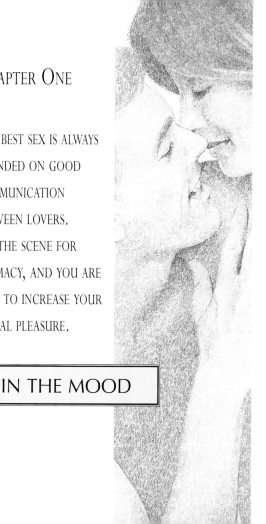

IN THE MOOD

Flirting

It starts with having fun together, then looks and body language show you're both in the mood for love–but first comes the thrill of the chase.

You are at your most erotic when you are magnetic; pull your partner towards you through the delicious art of flirting. With a smile, provocative eye contact, a whisper, or an unexpected but intimate touch, you can gently tease your partner to arousal; after all, flirting is the beginning of foreplay. It gives your partner titillating signals that you are ripe for seduction, and you are inviting them to play. Flirting adds spice to the art of lovemaking, and can make a woman feel more feminine, a man more masculine.

So much can be conveyed through initial eye contact

Creating the perfect sensual and sexual atmosphere for both of you is a wonderful way to start making love, and is certain to enhance your pleasure. Establishing the right mood helps create the excitement, and as the desire builds, so does that eager anticipation of the special sexual closeness that lies ahead. The most potent sexual organ of all is the brain. It is the source of your sexual creativity and imagination, so use it to the full!

Feeling good

Learn what arouses your partner. Then you can create a sizzling, sensual atmosphere.

Skin to skin contact will awaken your sexuality

9

Turn your partner on

Slowly, sensually undressing each other is guaranteed to light a fire between you.

You are sure to arouse your man if you undress him when you're already, enticingly, undressed yourself. He can feast his eyes on your body, appreciating what he sees now and savoring thoughts of what's to come. Meanwhile, you can lingeringly remove his clothing, a piece at a time, while kissing, stroking, and

Tease your partner by undressing him slowly

licking his body. Change the pace occasionally; you can undress him provocatively and slowly one time, and passionately, hurriedly tear off his clothes, unable to stem your lust, another! A woman, too, enjoys the arousing effect of slowly being undressed, as a tender lover unbuttons, unwraps, and unzips her clothes. For example, a man can lift her panties away from her labia,

or her bra from her breasts, after kissing her through the thin material. Then he may kiss her inner thighs while pulling her panties down. Pull them, teasingly, back up, between her buttocks. Caress her there, then either slide the panties off, or pull the elastic to one side and enter her, stroking her body as you do so.

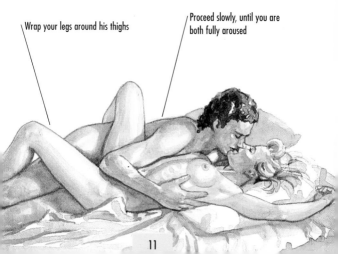

Wrap your legs around his thighs

Proceed slowly, until you are both fully aroused

Setting

Sex is the ultimate sensual experience, so create an atmosphere that arouses all the five senses of you and your partner.

Create the right setting for love by combining the smell of scented candles or flowers with the taste of good wine. Make sure you can hear the background sound of soft or throbbing music (whichever turns you both on). Combine it with the sight of an inviting log fire. Watch the flickering light as it plays on your naked bodies, lying in a shadowy room, whether you are on a softly textured sofa, or luxurious carpet, or between crisply ironed sheets.

Fantasize as you make love—it will add a passionate dimension

The most erotic atmosphere for sexual pleasure is created with your partner's tastes in mind—the best sexual partner is the one who gives better than he or she gets. The time, effort, and the imagination spent setting the scene for lovemaking is always worth it. Remember, too, sex does not have to be confined to the bedroom; consider using every other room in your home. (Or, perhaps you would enjoy taking your lusty playmate outside, to a secluded spot on the beach or in a forest.)

Talking & intimacy

Good communication, as well as sexy talk, is a sure way for you both to increase your sexual pleasure.

lovemaking, to reading aloud from erotic literature. Honeyed words make your lover feel desirable, and therefore more aroused.
Your pleasure can also be expressed in sounds, such as moans and sighs, which may inflame you both. And don't forget that the ear is an erogenous zone!

Sexy talk is like verbal foreplay, and some call it aural sex. The human voice is a powerful aphrodisiac. It can vary from whispering softly to your partner just what and how you feel during

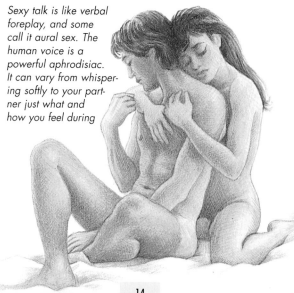

Chapter Two

BEFORE YOU ENJOY
FULL INTERCOURSE,
MANY TECHNIQUES
CAN PRODUCE
INTENSE EROTIC
FEELINGS–SAVOR
THEM FULLY.

FABULOUS FOREPLAY

Kissing & caressing

Savor the satisfaction of kissing and sensual play–it isn't just a prelude to love, but a highly pleasurable experience on its own!

There is no such thing as foreplay–only play. The idea that it is only a warm up, an appetizer, something that prepares you for the Big Event–intercourse–means you lose the enormous, overwhelming satisfaction that comes from kissing, teasing, and caressing. Savor the pleasure of sensuality–lose your senses in it! Because all the activity before intercourse is not foreplay, it's sex. And the longer you make the fun last, the more thrilling it will be.

Kissing is one of the crucial ingredients in good love-

making, lasting as it does through foreplay, intercourse and afterplay! Not only is your mouth an erogenous zone, but every inch of your partner's skin can become one, too, under your expert lips and tongue.

Particularly sensitive to kissing, licking, and sucking are the areas where the pulse is felt and the skin is thin: wrists, inside elbows and knees, armpits, the nape of the neck, and inner thighs. While your mouth is busy, your hands are free to caress the rest of your lover's body. Vary the pace of your stroking, from feathery touches and gentle caresses to firm massage, even light scratches.

Teasingly keep the genitals waiting for their share of attention. That way you will prolong the excitement!

Vary your kissing style, from a gentle caress to ardent kisses; it will keep your partner's arousal at fever pitch

Kissing & licking

Use your tongue to arouse your partner to the heights of sexual pleasure.

tongue stroke next? Vary your stroke—one minute, give soft little licks like a cat (for even better effect, dry your tongue beforehand with a towel, so it feels raspy on the skin), the next minute, long, wet strokes.

Genital kissing is the most intimate, as well as arousing,

One of the best ways to sharpen your partner's skin response is with the element of surprise—where will your

The mouth can be used in many creative ways!

kind. When kissing your partner's penis, pay lots of attention to his testicles, and the area between them and his anus. Your "cat" licks can be effective here. Your tongue can also probe, circle a sensitive area, caress, and even tickle. And, you can follow the path of your tongue with a trail of tender, gentle kisses.

The extra attention to your partner's skin and sensual areas makes him or her feel particularly pampered, and they are sure to give you some special pleasure at another time. When a man kisses his lover, he can start planting kisses around, then on the labia, then, gently, the clitoris, mimicking with his lips and tongue what she may do with her fingers to excite herself. He can put a pillow under her to raise her hips, for better access. He can probe gently, expertly with his tongue, softly blowing on the wet skin.

Kissing can also serve as a "second penetration"; parallel the rhythm of pelvic thrusting with that of your tongue for added excitement.

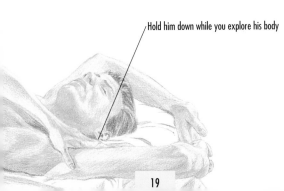
Hold him down while you explore his body

Stroking & touching

The art of touching is central to a satisfying sexual experience.

The sensual, erotic, primal pleasure of touch! The truly expert lover understands and uses touch's power, having first learned their partner's preferences.

Some people, in some places, prefer a feathery touch, others like a firmer one, still others respond to strong pressure. And desire for a certain touch can change, depending on mood, arousal, temperature, time of day, and even time of month.

Use your hands to familiarize yourself with every inch of your partner's body—slowly, thoroughly. Explore the silky hot skin where thigh meets groin, the rough texture of his hairy chest, the slippery smoothness of her labia, the firmness of a muscle, the intriguing bump of an erect nipple, the soft roundness of a buttock...

Caress with your hands, your nails, your lips, and your tongue. Be sensitive to the tiniest reaction of your partner's skin in response to gentle strokes, light scratches, or nibbles. The shudder of ecstacy, the small pull away from or toward you, tells you what to do next.

Touch can excite, electrify, soothe—it is the most powerful form of sexual contact!

Experiment with different touch sensations: stroke your partner with a fake fur mitt, a loofah, or a swansdown powder puff, and see how they respond.

The expert lover knows the power of constantly keeping body contact. Try rhythmically caressing her breast or his testicles after making love, as you both fall asleep in each other's arms.

Run your tongue down her rib cage

Close your eyes and focus on the sensations

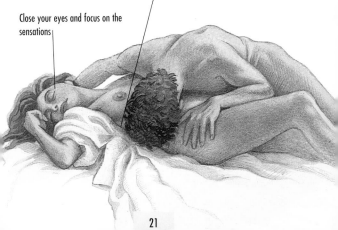

Massage can be a part of lovemaking, or done simply for relaxation, not conditional upon having sex. Either way, it is a great way of learning what your partner likes.

Awaken him, on a weekend morning, with tender caresses. Then, using oil warmed between your palms, turn him on his back, and use long, firm strokes to massage his body. Work down from his shoulders to his chest, stomach, arms,

Massage

Among its many benefits, massage helps loving couples build intimacy and trust—prime ingredients for terrific sex.

and legs. Unless he's ticklish, don't forget his feet. Apply firm pressure under the ball of his foot and around his toes. Turn him on his stomach, and leisurely, firmly, massage his shoulders and back, where tension can build up. Work down, as before, varying your

Relax, and let your head rest against your arms

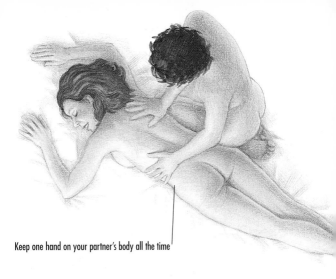

Keep one hand on your partner's body all the time

strokes as you go, pushing down in circles with your palms, or with your finger-tips, or knuckles for more specific pressure.

Men can massage women in the same way. With soft music playing in the back-ground, your cool hands on her warm flesh can make massage the most exquisite experience. Use perfumed body oil; the scent will arouse and delight her.

Gently combine long, firm strokes with smaller, circular movements, never letting your hands break contact with her skin.

Pay special attention to her breasts, shoulders, and back. Tell her how desirable you find her, and let your fingers stray between her buttocks and her thighs, to gently massage her labia. What she feels like doing next, is, of course, up to her...!

Masturbation

Partners can learn what their lovers like best if they watch each other masturbate.

Inviting your partner to watch you masturbate is a good way for them to see how you like to be aroused. It can also be exciting for them to play the voyeur. Indulge your fantasies about being slyly observed (or even being in front of a large audience!) as you devote yourself to your own orgasm. The total lack of inhibition results, too, in increased experimentation, which can lift your sex life to thrilling new heights. Or try mutual masturbation; your partner's orgasmic sounds can be an erotic soundtrack to your own climax!

Most men can achieve a second climax more quickly from your inventive hands than from entering you again. You can both have a lot of fun as you find out exactly how to make this happen.

> Use your hands either as a prelude to lovemaking, or as an enjoyable way of satisfying your lover when full intercourse is not possible.

Use a firm, pumping action on his penis

Let your lover lean against you as you take his penis in your hand. With you in control, he can really let himself relax.

Practice on him deliberately, relentlessly, until you find the rhythm that slows him down, keeping him in fever-pitch anticipation, or speeds him up, as he approaches his climax. Use both hands, one pressing hard near the base, holding his penis steady, or caressing his testicles. With the other hand, you can either make a ring with your thumb and forefinger, or wrap your whole hand around the shaft of his penis. He can then wrap his hand around yours, to guide you as you give him an explosive orgasm. Watching him ejaculate can add to your erotic pleasure.

In general, a woman prefers a light stroke on her clitoris, and firmer strokes around it, increasing speed as her excitement builds.

Let her guide your hand as she shows you what she likes: circular movements, perhaps, or up-and-down rubbing.

She can close her eyes and give in to whatever sexy images enter her mind, or watch your loving hand guide her to ecstasy. Try wearing a leather glove, or using a well-aimed shower head to create extra sensations. Tell her how much you delight in her, and find out what to do to help build her orgasm.

Urge your lover on with erotic dialogue, or, if she prefers, stay silent, while your tongue caresses her skin.

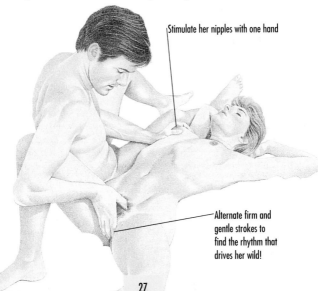

Stimulate her nipples with one hand

Alternate firm and gentle strokes to find the rhythm that drives her wild!

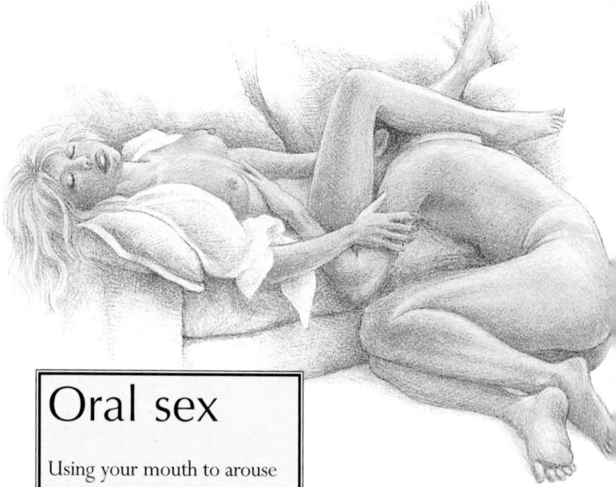

Oral sex

Using your mouth to arouse
your lover's body is a
natural part of lovemaking.

Both sexes should take note
of what their partner does
during oral sex–people usually do to others what they
would most like to have
done to them.

 When making love to a
woman, try gently lapping
her clitoris with your tongue,
then, as she becomes more
aroused, use the tip of your
tongue to probe around,
and lightly on, it. Take your
time, before concentrating
on the clitoris as your lover
approaches orgasm.

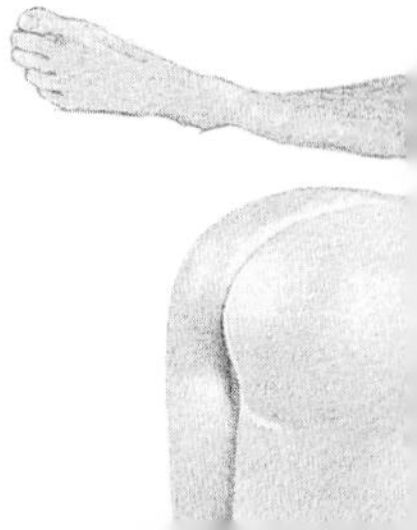

You can spice up your love play with food. Drizzle her with cream before bringing her to a climax, or a woman can dip her lover's penis in flavored liqueur or honey to lick off as lovemaking starts. When giving a man oral sex, run your tongue from the base to the tip and all around his penis, then tease the area between his penis and anus. Dive down the length of his shaft and suck, moving your head around and up and down, so he enjoys several sensations at once. Keep the pressure firm. Your rhythm should be slightly unpredictable, to add excitement. Move your hand up his shaft as your mouth goes down on it. And remember—oral sex can be extra fun when it's a quickie. Make it a hit-and-run affair!

Suck, flick, and swirl your tongue on and around your lover's penis

Mutual oral sex can be even more exciting when you're familiar with your partner's responses. It does mean you pay less attention to your own orgasm, because you're also focussed on your partner's. Side by side, or with one partner on top, are two popular positions. Both have advantages, but when the woman is on top she can have better control of his thrusting. He also has a great view of her buttocks.

To avoid a stiff neck if you are underneath, support yourself with pillows. While both mouths are busy, hands are free to caress the buttocks, or to part her labia, making way for a warm tongue. A finger can also be inserted into her vagina, or his anus, for more stimulation.

While facing each other side by side, each partner can pull up the under thigh, to rest the other's head. Pause when you like, but maintain contact with your hands.

Generally, a woman takes longer to reach a climax than a man, so she should vary her caresses, to slow him down, and he can try to time his orgasm to hers.

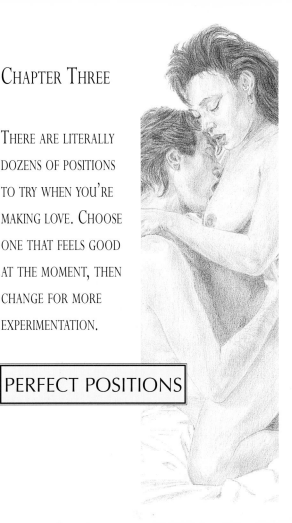

CHAPTER THREE

THERE ARE LITERALLY
DOZENS OF POSITIONS
TO TRY WHEN YOU'RE
MAKING LOVE. CHOOSE
ONE THAT FEELS GOOD
AT THE MOMENT, THEN
CHANGE FOR MORE
EXPERIMENTATION.

PERFECT POSITIONS

Missionary

All lovers enjoy this lovemaking position, with good reason, because it allows you to caress each other face to face.

There are many positions for making love, varying the amounts of eye contact, clitoral stimulation, and angle and depth of penetration.

Do what feels good for both of you at the time, but as you approach orgasm, it's a good idea to switch to another position that will let you relax completely.

The missionary position is a romantic and adaptable one, good for leisurely lovemaking or for quickie sex. To make sex even hotter in

this position, ensure the man's foreskin, if he has one, is peeled back. If his partner ripples her vaginal muscles, she can increase his arousal. She can also slow him down, if she needs more time to reach orgasm, by relaxing those muscles, so there's less pressure on his penis from the vaginal wall.

The man can please his lover by making his thrusts shallow; most nerve endings in the vagina lie near the outside of the body.

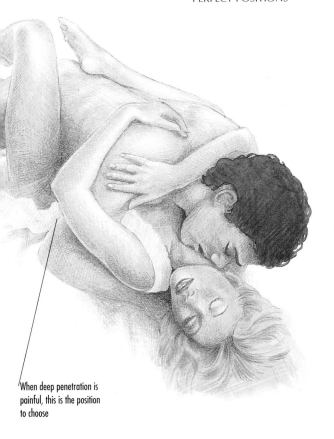

When deep penetration is
painful, this is the position
to choose

X-position

It's the weekend, you have plenty of time. The telephone is off the hook. Now is the time to enjoy your sensuality. See how much pleasure you can get from this exciting position!

They both lean back. They can hold each other's hands for balance, or they can lean on their hands behind them, giving extra leverage. By coordinating wiggling and contracting movements,

This interesting position is very good for extended, leisurely intercourse. And a slight adjustment of a leg here, or a hip there, can make subtle differences in the sensations you feel.
  The woman sits astride her man, face to face, with one leg under his thigh, and the other resting on his shoulder. His penis is completely inserted, which puts the maximum pressure on the front of her vaginal wall.

he will remain fully erect, and she will feel highly aroused, for a long period of time. To change to another position, perhaps one more direct and comfortable that will release the pent-up

orgasm, both partners can sit up, without disengaging from each other.

Lean back, and experiment with the different sensations you can produce from slight changes in position

Your touch will let him know how you feel

Man
on top

This is ideal when a woman does not feel like taking control, or when she wants gentle lovemaking.

When a man positions himself on top of his lover, she can guide his penis toward her vaginal entrance. In this position she can pause in the middle of making love, and stroke her partner's hair, or caress his back, before resuming action!
 The woman can straighten her legs and keep them together, so her man's legs lie outside hers. As he

squeezes her thighs with his own, her thighs snugly squeeze his inserted penis, for extra friction.

In this position a woman can change the degree of penetration by bringing her thighs closer to her chest. Playing with pillows allows lovers to find extra leverage, or to experiment with how high he rides her (for more clitoral stimulation, she can hold her vaginal lips a bit wider), or where he positions her arms. He can also place one leg between hers, or use his fingers to massage her clitoris.

Her thigh can rub against his testicles, which can be even more arousing. While he is on top, she can lie halfway onto her side so his entry is half-top, half-rear, for a good variation of sensation.

Move your leg up and down to change the depth of penetration

Deep penetration

To achieve ultimate sexual satisfaction, experiment with a variety of positions and movements.

For satisfying depth of entry, a woman can, with legs raised, push her hips forward at the deepest point of *her lover's stroke. As his pubic bone rubs against her clitoris, she will experience additional stimulation. For even deeper penetration, she can wrap her legs around his waist. He can also, with a hand around each of her ankles, lift her legs over her head, then enter her, using more of his weight behind each thrust.*

By opening her legs wider, as well as raising them, the woman can help her man direct his penis at a more acute angle, and his thrusts will reach deeper inside. She might even feel the head of his penis touching the neck of her cervix. Some women find their cervix is too sensitive for this to be enjoyable, while others find it very arousing. The woman can lower her head and upper body over the edge of the bed, but she should be careful so both partners feel safe and comfortable.

A man can achieve very deep penetration by entering his lover from behind

Woman on top

This wonderfully versatile way to make love is sure to get a woman aroused.

In this position a woman can lean forward to have her breasts or mouth kissed, or for more clitoral stimulation and less penetration. She can sit straight up for really deep insertion, or lean back to display her body to her partner's gaze.

A woman can also massage her own clitoris. To prolong the pleasure, she can move away sometimes. If she wants to rest, she can lie with her legs between, or on each side of, her partner's legs.

If the woman squats over her lover, his frenulum (an exquisitely sensitive area of skin that extends from underneath his shaft to his glans) will be extrastimulated against the back of her vagina, which is very arousing! She can add to this by contracting and relaxing her vaginal muscles.

While she is on top, he can massage her clitoris and her breasts. She can also reverse her position, so she sits with her back and buttocks facing him, for another erotic view.

Be guided by your partner, respond to her sounds and movements

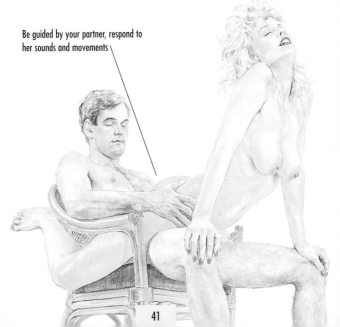

Rear entry

Exciting sensations will delight you and your partner when you make love in this fashion.

Many women like the feeling of being taken from behind, but there is a lack of face-to-face contact here, so you miss out on kissing. In compensation, you gain pleasure from the extra caressing of the buttocks and back.

If the "animal-like" feeling of man-behind, rear-entry sex turns your woman off, the position shown below is a good alternative. She has more control, and she can offer a variety of sensations for you both, by rocking back and forth. You can stimulate her breasts and

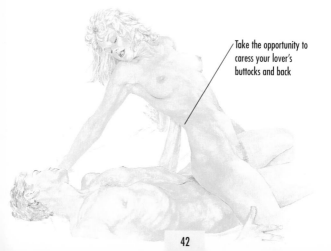

Take the opportunity to caress your lover's buttocks and back

her pubic mound, for an orgasm of more dif-fused intensity than is usually experienced through direct clitoral massage. Like all rear-entry positions, this one is comfortable during pregnancy.

The "doggy-style" position keeps the man's hands free, so he can caress his lover's body.

A man should take care not to enter his lover too deeply, because he may bump an ovary with his penis. (That can hurt as much as a jabbed testicle.)

The woman can also lean over, with her hands on the edge of the bed, as her partner enters her, holding her legs by the knees, for a subtle difference in sensation.

This position is a good one for deep penetration. However, if your lover is kneeling on the bed as you enter her, be careful not to thrust so hard that her head is pushed down so she can't breathe.

Sideway

Savor the pleasure of side-entry sex—it offers a great sense of intimacy, as well as the opportunity for deep thrusting by the man.

In the half-sideway position, the woman turns her back to her lover with her knees raised, and he inserts his penis. Alternatively, she can put one of her legs between his, allowing him to thrust even deeper. The position is also good for intimacy, as his face is close to hers.

While one of the man's arms is used for balance, the other can caress his lover's breasts. Then, by slipping in beside her, so they are in the "spoons" position, without pulling out, he has access to her clitoris. It is a restful, close position.

Cuddle up to your lover's back to create a feeling of greater intimacy

Using a chair

All kinds of props can add thrills to your love life—for resourceful lovers a chair is just the start.

Seated positions take the strain off the man, although they do limit his pelvic movement. He can grasp the woman's hips, however, as she leans back, gripping the chair arms. Together they can maneuver her for the most arousing penetration, while he firmly massages her pubic mound, matching the movement to his own rhythm.

Alternatively, the woman can sit in the chair, raising herself a little by holding the arms. Her man stands facing her, and lifts her buttocks as he enters her, also enjoying an erotic, full-body view.

Stroke your lover's anus and perineum; they are erotically sensitive areas ———

New positions

You've tried the rest—now is the time to experiment! Try these suggestions, and see where they lead you.

One of the keys to fulfilling lovemaking is a willingness to try new positions, or even to invent your own.

You'll find some positions impede movement, or are difficult to get into, but they might offer instead a new angle of penetration, and enjoyable new sensations!

In the position shown here, the woman lies at the edge of the bed, with her legs raised. The man kneels astride her, facing her feet, then enters her. He leans toward the floor as she lies back. He supports himself, and his lover caresses his buttocks as he thrusts.

By switching positions mid-way through lovemaking, both partners can enjoy taking advantage of the many differing sensations a variety of movement brings. They also ensure fun remains a vital ingredient in their lives! In the illustration on this page, the man has sufficient penetration for a satisfying orgasm, and both he and his partner are in a good position to stimulate her clitoris, giving extra pleasure.

Caress her legs, stomach, and thighs, and enjoy looking at her at the same time. She is free to pleasure herself, so you can concentrate on your own orgasm.

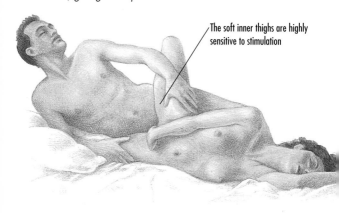

The soft inner thighs are highly sensitive to stimulation

CHAPTER FOUR

EVERYDAY SEX IS GREAT,
BUT FROM TIME TO
TIME LOVEMAKING CAN
BE EXTRA SENSATIONAL.
YOU WILL REMEMBER
THOSE EXCITING TIMES
WITH SPECIAL DELIGHT.

MAKING SEX MEMORABLE

Treating your lover

You can turn up the heat in your relationship by forgetting about orgasms and concentrating on the sensations of lovemaking.

Sex is not a performance, so don't feel you have to prove what a great lover you are. Simply by giving pleasure to each other, perhaps for hours, you can refresh the sensual aspects of good sex. Love for the moment, as you live it, not for the finish.

By taking time over each tiny caress, and carefully noticing your partner's responses, you could re-familiarize yourselves with what turns you both on.

Communication helps, as does a sense of humor and the desire to give.

The sexual ego is a fragile thing, so fire up each other's fantasies, and make your partner feel like the most desirable, sexy person in the world! When they feel good they will want to make you feel good, and that makes sex unforgettable!

Making someone feel sexy works, of course, both ways. A woman can do much to guarantee her sexual pleasure by appreciating that the male sexual reponse is fired up by visual stimulus. She should make the most of sexy clothing that displays her assets well (see page 74). And men should never forget that, for most women, tenderness is an important part of good sex.

Let him know how you feel about what he is doing—small gasps and moans will tell him a lot

Listen to your partner, and respond to her movements

Additional treats

Show your partner how much you care, and your sex life will really sizzle!

A woman who wants sensational sex should find out what gets her man erotically excited, then try to fulfil those needs. That way both partners can enjoy a hotter, more satisfying sex life.
Men tend to get into "the mood" along the genital , rather than the emotional route. So a man's lover can feel confident about initiating sex play, which is not only arousing for him, but also takes the pressure off him to always "be the one".

Enjoy caressing her buttocks as you thrust into her from behind.

Close your eyes and concentrate on the erotic sensations

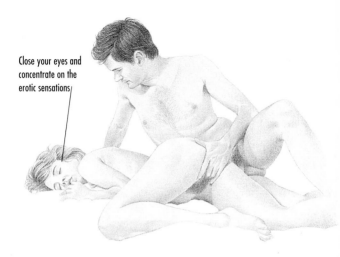

A man will find his partner wonderfully responsive if he can make her feel reaching an orgasm is not the main goal of lovemaking. It is the loving that precedes orgasm, especially with her, that she wants to feel is important.

Many women think sexual technique is not as important as affection and a desire to make her satisfied. The man who can make his partner feel wildly sexy, desirable, and cared for is considered the best lover.

He can give her oral sex for more than one orgasm, for example, or caress her tenderly not only before, but during and after lovemaking. And, remember, the good lover doesn't just roll over to sleep because he's through!

Sexy vacations

With your everyday cares behind you, now is the ideal time for love.

Every now and then, refresh your lovemaking pattern by changing locations. The combination of a different setting and vacation relaxation can work wonders! Try a secluded beach (or semisecluded, for an extra thrill), or the woods, or even a motel room for the night; keep an eye open for places that could turn your vacation into an erotic playground. Whether it's exotic winds blowing through your hair,

54

tropical sun shining on your skin, or a beautiful bed in a motel room, use it as a perfect opportunity to explore new erotic territory.

Not only are people more relaxed on vacation, they're also more adventurous. Being in a foreign locale can bring out nuances in personality–enjoy being somebody different in lovemaking, as well.

Vacation sex doesn't have to be planned. It can be a spontaneous day out, or a weekend in a country inn. Leave the kids with friends, and get to know your exotic, erotic selves again.

> You're on vacation, so don't resist the mood for love and adventure. Make the most of free time to have fun together, and rediscover the joys of uninhibited sex.

Brace yourself against a stool, so your lover can thrust into you

Quickie sex

You want each other passionately, *NOW*. Where and how are you going to make love?

The sudden, irresistible burst of lust can take over any time and any place–almost–so don't resist! Quickie sex has a different feel to it: animal-like, brief, strong, urgent, and hurried, and often high-ly pleasurable!

Both partners need to be equally aroused. Quickies are best when it's a wordless bolt of inspiration between the two of you. There's no time to get completely undressed, or settle into a relaxing position. So enjoy it, with your clothes pulled up or down, just enough,

while you are sitting, standing, or kneeling, depending
on where the urge takes you.
Spontaneous sex means los-
ing your inhibitions; if you
initiate it, your partner feels
they're so sexy you can't
help yourself, you have to
have them–now this minute.
If the man has often been
the main initiator in the
past, it's especially flattering
and arousing for him if his
lover takes the lead for a
change. Quick sex can also
bring him great satisfaction
if he is used to prolonged
foreplay sessions, with his
partner's arousal foremost
in his mind.

Caress each other's buttocks
while you enjoy sex standing up

Dress in the way you know will turn him on

If quickie sex could be on the menu, make sure you're dressed thrillingly–so you can be undressed quickly! Leave your underwear off altogether, or wear sexy crotchless panties, or maybe a front-opening bra. Don't wear layers of clothing, and be sure to wear items that can be easily pulled up or down or off, and rearranged by your impatient lover in a flash.

Leave the tantalizing tease of buttons, zippers, and hooks for another time. Wear silky, fine stockings, and garter belts instead of your usual panty-hose.

A favorite fantasy with both sexes is taking and being taken in an unlikely spot, where discovery is an imminent danger–that can make sex memorable, too, and account for some of the most thrilling orgasms.

The back seat of the car? Behind the door at a party? Or stuck in the elevator? Sharpen your eyes, as well as your imagination, for likely opportunities.

And don't forget home ground. What about while your partner is dressing for work? Use the closet door for support. Bending over the oven or a desk? Perfect! Try the kitchen table or the hallway stairs: the possibilities are endless!

Close your eyes and indulge in sexual fantasies as he enters you from behind

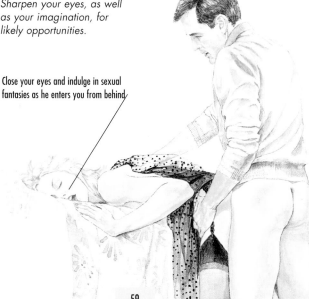

G-spot

Some experts claim it does not exist, but if you can find this hidden area inside the vagina, you will add an extra thrill to your lovemaking.

The G-spot is a small mass of tissue, the size of a pea, located inside the vaginal opening, on its front wall. It is reputedly an erogenous zone, which, when it is stimulated, swells and provides a unique reaction, different from the usual clitoral orgasm.

The G-spot's existence is still questioned, but many women notice that some areas of their vagina are more sensitive to erotic touch than others.

To experiment with finding your lover's G-spot, use one or two fingers, in a "come here" motion, against the inside roof of her vagina, about one third of the way up. Play with the finger pressure and the location for the most arousing response.

During lovemaking, she should kneel down on the bed, her buttocks raised as high as possible with legs widely apart, as her partner inserts his penis. For an even stronger climax, she can keep one hand free to press on the G-spot area from the outside, for extra stimulation.

With the woman on top of her lover, she can control the direction and depth of his penis

His orgasm

Find out what he needs to be fully aroused and enjoy a really explosive orgasm.

To arouse your man, get to know what he likes. Does he have a favorite position, enjoy oral sex, or playing different roles? Your relationship can ascend to new heights when you know secret ways to please him. Try placing a lubricated finger in his anus, which is erotically very sensitive. Massaging his prostate gland with your finger while stroking his perineum can provide a wonderful climax. Give your man his most explosive orgasm by caressing his penis (with your hand or mouth) just before the point of no return, then

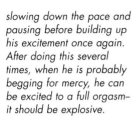

slowing down the pace and pausing before building up his excitement once again. After doing this several times, when he is probably begging for mercy, he can be excited to a full orgasm– it should be explosive.

Give him a "trip around the world", starting off with his penis, then licking his testicles, licking and probing the anus and perineum, then back to his penis again.

Make sure you are comfortable, so you can concentrate fully on your lover

Her orgasm

Enjoy the satisfaction of bringing her to the point of orgasm several times before you take her to the final, thrilling climax!

Because few women climax after thrusting alone, the sensitive man needs to find out what else his partner needs. She may have her favorite positions, ones that offer her the freedom of movement she wants.

To avoid painful friction, she should be well lubricated. He can thrust sideways, instead of just straight in and out, to give her even more stimulation.
She should be encouraged to reach her orgasm first, removing any pressure to be "the perfect lover" for him. Enthusiastic and loving oral sex, without an eye on the clock, is one of the most loving gestures a man can give. It also can provide a wonderful orgasm!

He can whisper in her ear (an erotically sensitive area) how beautiful he finds her body, while he strokes her breasts, neck, inner thighs, and anus, or massages her labia and clitoris. Try arousing her almost to the point of orgasm, then slowing down. Do this several times, until you finally bring her to a shattering climax. If a woman wants more, she may

Your woman may need more time than you to reach an orgasm; tell her she has all the time in the world

go on to a second or even third orgasm. You should be happy to oblige–but listen to the signals she gives you to find out when you can resume oral sex and when it would be too painful.

Simultaneous orgasms

This doesn't need to be your main goal when making love, but it's sensational when it happens.

Climaxing together is a real cooperative effort, because neither partner can be as spontaneous as if they were able to focus solely on their own

orgasm. Both orgasms can be increased by muscular contractions happening in the other's body while one person is climaxing.

Becoming familiar with the techniques and rhythms each one uses makes it easier for lovers to have a simultaneous explosion of pleasure. His penis, for example, may stiffen and his testicles tighten just before ejaculation, while her hardening nipples and the contractions inside her vagina tell when she's just at the point of coming.

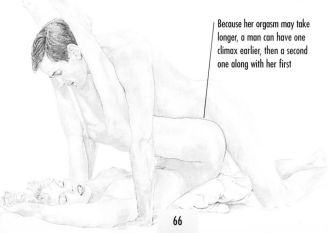

Because her orgasm may take longer, a man can have one climax earlier, then a second one along with her first

CHAPTER FIVE

THE MIND IS YOUR
MOST IMPORTANT
EROGENOUS ZONE. USE
IT TO THE FULL AND
YOUR LOVE LIFE WILL
REALLY TAKE OFF!

USE YOUR IMAGINATION

Fantasies

A loving couple will enjoy sharing a rich fantasy life. Tell each other your desires and inner dreams—it will bring you even closer together.

Bedtime—or where and whenever you have your sexual adventures–is the perfect opportunity to explore all the sexy fantasies, games, and ideas you have ever wanted to try. After all, sex should be fun, as well as loving and passionate. The

only rule is that both partners should enter any games willingly; sex should not hurt, upset, or victimize anyone. That aside, let loose your creative imagination. No matter how wild the thought, with a willing partner, anything goes! The sophisticated lover encourages a partner's fantasies, and the willingness to act them out, if desired. Heterosexual, homosexual, romantic, or wild, fantasies can become part of your love play–they don't have to happen in real life. It's a way of trying out new roles and should excite, not change or threaten. And, of course, indulging in fantasy can be the most erotically releasing experience!

A fantasy helps to release your essential erotic personality —

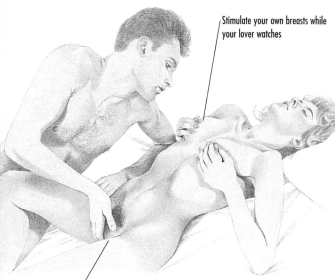

Stimulate your own breasts while your lover watches

Use firm pressure as she builds to a climax

Private daydreams can be especially useful if a woman has difficulty in reaching an orgasm. In her mind she can be a movie star, a character from a novel, or anyone she feels like. Fantasizing just before her climax can be arousing enough to keep her erotic sensations burning, strong and satisfying!

Try such favorites as being overpowered by a seductive villain, being catered to by four men at once, or watched by a lusting audience.

For even greater satisfaction, act out your fantasies with your lover. You can be the stars in your own pornographic film. Use colored lightbulbs (or cover a lamp with a fireproof scarf), an interesting background, and a camera. There's no problem in having mildly erotic photographs commercially developed, but use an instant camera for truly hot images.

The instant-replay camcorder is another useful tool. The zoom lens can be used for "special effects", as can the tripod, so both of you can be captured on film in all your sexual glory.

Throw back your head in passion

Spread your legs for the camera

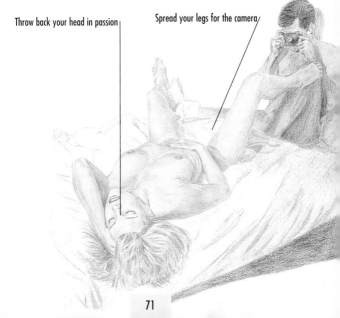

Many lovers find adding the illusion of anonymity to love-making provides an extra frisson to their sexual life. If you blindfold your partner, you allow them the opportunity to imagine a strange person's hands, lips, or genitals probing or caressing them—which can be very arousing! In addition, when you suppress one sense you sharpen others; after one partner is blindfolded, the other one can deliberately, slowly, explore every inch of their lover's body; all their sensations will be deliciously magnified.

Make your caresses different from usual—rougher, gentler—you will add to the sense of novelty

There's a bit of the voyeur in most of us, so double the erotic pleasure by making love in front of a mirror. Better yet, make that two or more mirrors! Both sexes can be strongly excited by seeing themselves orally stimulated, masturbated, or being taken in exotic positions.

The excitement is partly the result of seeing yourself as a desirable pinup or film star. The new experience will encourage you to lose your inhibitions, as you become absorbed in the role. And, your lover can seem like a stranger making love to you, another arousing scenario.

If you think the mirror won't flatter you, keep the lights dim at first—before long you won't care!

73

Dressing up

You can be as glamorous as a film star, or play a thousand different roles, when you dress for your lover's eyes only.

Sexy lingerie is a huge turn-on for most men; wearing it can also make a woman feel extra sexy, especially if her efforts are met with obvious approval. She can wear things that exaggerate specially female features. A small waist is emphasized by a pretty corset or a tight, curvy "body". Beautiful breasts and nipples are shown to advantage in a sexy half-cup, cut-out or sheer bra. Thongs, bikinis and G-strings display rounded buttocks and genitals, yet tantalizingly hide them from her lover at the same time.

Garter belts and stockings, worn with high-heels, can make a woman's legs seem longer and more shapely. Indeed, stockings emphasize her sexuality like nothing else.

Favorite colours of lingerie are naughty black, virgin white, and siren red; find out your man's preferences. Textures of lingerie and other sexy clothing add extra heat to the sensual power of touch. Silk is best for panties and G-strings; it's smooth, and soft, and holds the skin's scent better than synthetics. High heels (for her) and high boots (for both) are turn-ons for some people; patent leather is better than vinyl, because leather mimics human skin. If you like the look and smell of leather, buy a leather jockstrap for him, a leather-based perfume for her.

Use your sense of smell—it heightens erotic stimulation

Push rhythmically against him for added clitoral stimulation

Resourceful lovers can dress up... and down. Many men appreciate a good sexy striptease. Especially if you do it to sexy, rather than burlesque, music.

Slowly, mercilessly, remove one piece of clothing at a time, down to your sexy undies, then pull a bra strap down and lift out a breast from the cup. Tease down panties on one side, just to give a glimpse of what lies underneath, then pull them back up. Your lover can remove the rest, with hands tied behind his back–if he can do it! You could add to the illusion of being "another woman" by wearing a mask.

A man can please his partner by wearing tight jeans and a flannel shirt to play a rough workman, or knee-high boots, a whip and a frilly shirt to play the romantic hero.

Being partly dressed is more sexy than being naked: while dressing for a date, "forget" to put on some underwear. Only tell your partner after you are out–it will drive you both wild with desire!

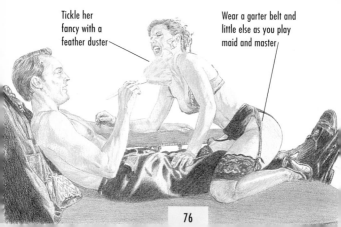

Tickle her fancy with a feather duster

Wear a garter belt and little else as you play maid and master

Try playing at being each other's love slave for an evening. Promise to fulfil any erotic request your lover makes, while you act as their sexual plaything.

A secret peep of a sexy, front-opening bra under a business jacket could be very arousing to your man. Unhook it, leaving it and the jacket open, and straddle your lover for quickie sex.
For a special occasion, create an Arabian night, using incense, pillows and rugs on the floor, with a backdrop of soft lights and Eastern music. The man plays Valentino, with costume (from a hire store), ready to conquer his woman with seductive, masterful ways. She, in sequined bra, jewelry and veils (to be removed, one at a time, in a dance), tantalizes and arouses him with a harem girl's skills.

Surprise her

Give her just what she likes when she least expects it, and you could be rewarded with some memorable lovemaking!

There are many ways to please a woman. Try some of the following and she is sure to respond.

Give your lover the most leisurely massage she's ever had. Don't stop until she's climaxed twice.

Buy her some silky lingerie. Leave an erotic, romantic love letter tucked under her pillow, to be found when she wakens. Or, in her purse, to be found at work.

Drizzle her body with warm honey and spend a long time licking it all off.

Kidnap her one weekend, and drive her to a hotel, where you have reserved a room, stocked with flowers and wine, for the night.

Or, show her you can't wait for bedtime, by taking her standing up in the kitchen!

Surprise him

Men love sexy surprises, too. Let him know you think he's the most desirable man in the world by giving him a special treat.

Your man will love it if you put his favorite fantasy on the night's program–without any warning.

If you wake him up at 3 a.m., kissing and caressing his penis.

Let your T-shirt get wet, as you pull him into the shower and soap him all over.

If you ring him at work, with sexy suggestions for the night.

Bathtime

The bathtub, filled with bubble bath or scented oils, is a perfect place for warming up together, or for passionate sex!

Bathing together brings you intimacy, as well as cleanliness. Have two glasses of wine within reach, and soft, fluffy bathtowels nearby, to wrap each other in after you are both clean and glowing. To start, each of you can rub soap all over, masturbating yourselves or each other.

Within the limited space of most bathtubs, the doggie position is an ideal one for lovers! Or, the man can lie back on his elbows while his lover straddles him, leaning back on his thighs, and putting her legs on his shoulders. Or, you can both just lie back and tell each other your fantasies, and decide what to do when you finally get to bed!

Showertime

Taking a steamy shower together is sure to enliven your love life.

Get yourselves in a lather as you give in to your passion for one another.

Showering in the dark, with perhaps one burning candle and sexy music in the background, can create an erotic atmosphere. Lather each other all over with soap, your hands can slide anywhere you feel like!

The shower is a great place to have oral sex. Kneel down and let your parner drown in passion.

Penetration is possible, too. Enter your woman as she stands with her back against the shower wall, and allow the warm water cascade down you both.

Remember—the floors of showers and bathrooms can be slippery with water. Put down a slip-proof mat if you are feeling extra passionate!

The food of love

No food is an aphrodisiac, but a delicious meal can make us ready for love. Eat well, but lightly, for energy, and to help you relax together.

If you're eating with your partner, and in a sexy mood, keep meals light and spicy, not rich and substantial.

Enjoy a naked bedtime feast, with fruit, crackers, hard-boiled eggs, or smoked salmon. Suck and lick suggestively on bananas, peaches, asparagus, figs–foods that are sexual in appearance. Think of it as foreplay!

To lust!

Turn on with your favorite tipple—wine, ice-cold champagne, or peach juice.

A glass or two of alcohol strips away inhibitions—any more relaxes a man's penis as well, so for great sex don't indulge too much. You can save flavored liqueurs for drizzling on hot bodies. Lick them sensuously off eager labia, or a throbbing penis. Or, drink drops of sparkling champagne from sensitive points of the body.

Sex toys

They can't replace humans, but sex toys are fun and inexpensive treats to bring into the bedroom. And make sure you remember your sense of humor!

For women, sex toys can provide added stimulation before intercourse, or can be used to help achieve an explosive orgasm.

Japanese love balls are two plastic spheres, one hollow, the other weighted, connected by a cord. They can be inserted into the vagina. The balls shift about and vibrate, giving stimulation as the woman moves around. They are used more for novelty than effect, but some women do gain some enjoyment from them.

The love egg is another toy, also with a cord. It contains a vibrator, and can either be placed on the clitoris or in the vagina.

Vibrators are great for
arousing the clitoris, which
is often not stimulated enough
during intercourse.

Many vibrators are penis-
shaped, and can be inserted
into a woman's vagina, or
the anus of either partner. If
the sensation is too strong, a
thin towel wrapped around

the vibrator will absorb
some shock waves!

Dildoes are artificial penises,
which can be useful if your
lover's erection has softened.
Penile extenders are sheaths
adding more than an inch
to the penis length–beneficial
if a woman likes deep penetration during intercourse.

Sexy games

All games are fun. But these raunchy lovers' games are strictly for the grownups!

If sex games intrigue you, they can add humor and enjoyment to your erotic relationship. Why not transform a pack of cards into a game of strip poker? As each partner removes one piece of clothing or jewelry at a time, it's a teasing bit of foreplay. And, you can have fun as the winner demands a sexual "forfeit" from the loser.

Or play "Sex Scrabble", where each word must be sexual in nature–with the most interesting words acted out by the loser, later.

Almost any game, from one on a board to one in your imagination, can be played for sexy stakes. The penalty is levied by the winner. They might demand an erotic massage, an hour of non-stop oral sex, or a kind of position they have fantasized about, but have never dared ask their partner to try.

Or make your fantasies part of the game. Play slave and master or mistress; boss and employee; doctor and nurse.

You can turn these fantasies into "forfeits or favors," which can add an extra thrill to the art of arousal. Whatever happens, you will both be the winners when you play sexy games.

Make him undress you as one of his sexual "forfeits"—he won't complain

Bondage

This is not a way to force yourself on your lover. But it can be a help for him or her to achieve an orgasm.

This enormously popular sexual fantasy frees both men's and women's occasional impulse either to dominate and control–or to be overpowered and submissive. The desire and the pretence is mutual.

Bind your lover with scarves, ribbons, pajama sashes, or soft ropes (with easy-to-undo knots)–even a dog's leash or leather harness can be used, for real control. Bondage is good for expert, slow masturbation–your lover will be helpless in your hands. Or, a woman can tie her partner down while she brings herself to orgasm; watching and not being able to move can be highly arousing to many men.

Light S&M

Mild sadomasochism is wonderful for sex-role switching, which can be highly arousing in itself.

their body. The idea is often more erotic than the reality, so enjoy the trappings, such as whips, or a riding crop, but do not use them as more than a provocative gesture.

If you want to go farther, remember the awareness of pain decreases with arousal, so be careful.

Consider mild S & M–light spanking, perhaps, or tying your partner's arms to the showerhead, then using the nozzle to run a hard spray of warm water all over

After setting a few ground rules, such as signals when "enough" really does mean enough, putting one's body at the mercy of another can be a delicious feeling.

After tying wrists and perhaps ankles to the bedpost or frame, sensually stimulate every inch of your partner's body by stroking it with a variety of textures to awaken subtle and erotic sensations. Trail a soft feather boa, a piece of ice, or a dribble of just-hot-enough-to-surprise flavored oil across their skin. For a rougher texture, stroke his or her skin with a loofah, or your fingernails.

Surprise with an uneven weave of kisses and sharp nips, from head to feet, straddling, ever so slightly, the border between pleasure and pain. Rent a titillating video—and invent your own sexy games!

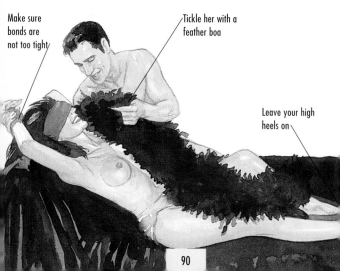

Make sure bonds are not too tight

Tickle her with a feather boa

Leave your high heels on

Chapter Six

Love doesn't have to end when you climax. Find out how to enjoy the tender time that comes after an orgasm.

AFTERWARDS

Afterwards

Express your feelings of togetherness in the quiet moments after passion.

happened. It's important to hear reassuring, complimentary words when still feeling vulnerable. Instead of rolling over or getting up, take time to enjoy the afterglow—and the simple pleasure of being with each other.

After your bodies have climaxed, the lovemaking should continue. It's a quiet, relaxing time, and a chance to caress each other gently and express affection, appreciation, and sheer enjoyment of what's just

Some people, particularly men, feel sleepy after sex. It's a good time to curl up lazily in each other's arms and prolong the wonderful feeling of closeness as you both drift slowly off to sleep. If you are feeling wide awake, however, refresh yourselves with a snack put by the bed beforehand. Easy-to-eat foods, such as croissants, cheeses, grapes, or sandwiches make perfect postpleasure pick-me-ups. Re-energized, you might find you want to carry on into the night...

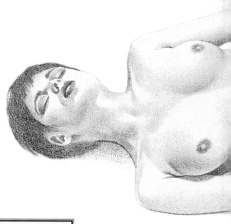

Start again

After love-making, your bodies will be relaxed and hypersensitive. Give your lover an all-over stroking, and who knows what might happen next?

Whether you start to make love again immediately, or wait until the warm moments after sleep in the morning, is up to you. The second round of love-making will probably be even more pleasurable for both of you

than the first, as you build upon the intense feelings of intimacy you've established. You may find the next time, when you are both relaxed and uninhibited, a good chance to try out new ways of arousing each other.

Listen to what your lover suggests and be willing to experiment with different caresses or games of love. Be gentle and take time to excite each other slowly, as you build up to another tumultuous climax.

INDEX